David and Goliath

Om KIDZ

An imprint of Om Books International

Saul, the King of Israel, was an unhappy man. In those days, the Israelites were fighting a war against the Philistines. He felt burdened by his responsibilities as a king. His weariness

and disobedience caused him to fall out of God's favour. God asked Samuel to go to Bethlehem and look for Jesse, one of whose eight sons was chosen to be the next king.

So Samuel went to Bethlehem and found the youngest of Jesse's children. The boy was called David. David was a shepherd boy who looked after his father's sheep. He played the harp beautifully.

David had three elder brothers in King Saul's army already. Samuel arranged for David to play the harp for Saul. The sweet music of the harp always calmed him down.

One day, the Israelite army put up their camp near the Valley of Elah. The Philistines were camping on the opposite hill.

Suddenly, a man called Goliath, came out of the Philistine camp. He was as huge as a giant. Dressed

in an armour for protection, he was also carrying an enormous spear.

Goliath's loud voice roared across the valley, "Servants of Saul, send a man to fight me. If he kills me, the Philistines will become your slaves, but if I win, you will become our slaves."

Everyone was quiet. The Israeli soldiers looked at each other, all of them afraid. The giant continued to do this for the next forty days.

He would come out and challenge the Israelites. King Saul promised a reward to anyone who would kill him, but no one came forward.

One day, David came to the camp to meet his brothers. He saw Goliath come out and shout. When he met the King, David told him, "Do not worry, I will defeat that giant."

King Saul was surprised. He asked, "How can you fight him when you are only a shepherd boy?"

David replied, "I have fought bears and lions that have tried to harm my sheep. The Lord will help me."

David took his sling and picked up five smooth stones from the stream in the valley.

The next day, when Goliath came out and saw his opponent David, he laughed loudly.

David was calm and said, "I fight in the name of the Lord and He will make me win."

Goliath became angry. He moved forward to attack David but David was very quick. He used his sling to shoot a stone that hit Goliath on the forehead. The giant fell, dead.

When they saw Goliath dead, the Philistine army fled away. The Israeli soldiers celebrated happily and David became a hero.